PINOCCHIO

Modern Curriculum Press
BEGINNING
TO
READ
Series

PINOCCHIO

Margaret Hillert

Illustrated by Laurie Hamilton

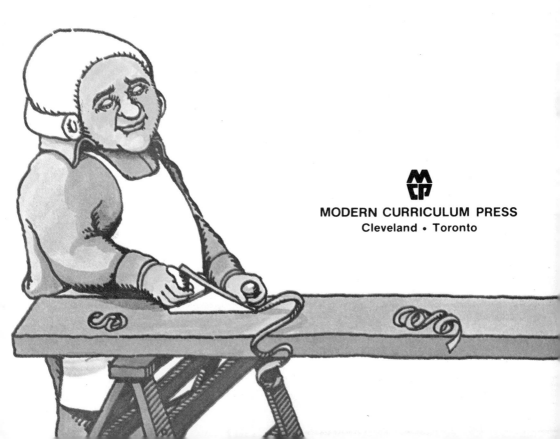

MODERN CURRICULUM PRESS
Cleveland • Toronto

Library of Congress Cataloging in Publication Data

Hillert, Margaret.
  Pinocchio.

  (MCP beginning-to-read books)

  SUMMARY: In Geppetto's hand a piece of wood
that talks becomes a living mischievous
marionette and eventually, after many trials and
errors, a real boy.
  [1. Fairy tales. 2. Puppets and puppet-plays —
Fiction] I. Lorenzini, Carlo, 1826-1890.
Avventure de Pinocchio. II. Hamilton, Laurie.
III. Title.
PZ8.H5425Pi   [E]   80-20843

ISBN 0-8136-5603-6 Paperback
ISBN 0-8136-5103-4 Hardbound

2 3 4 5 6 7 8 9 10
86 85 84

I want a little boy.
I will make one.
This is the way to do it.
Yes, yes.
I can make a boy.

Look here.
See this and this.
I can do it.
It looks pretty good.

Yes, yes.
Look at this.
Here is my little boy.
Oh, my. Oh, my.

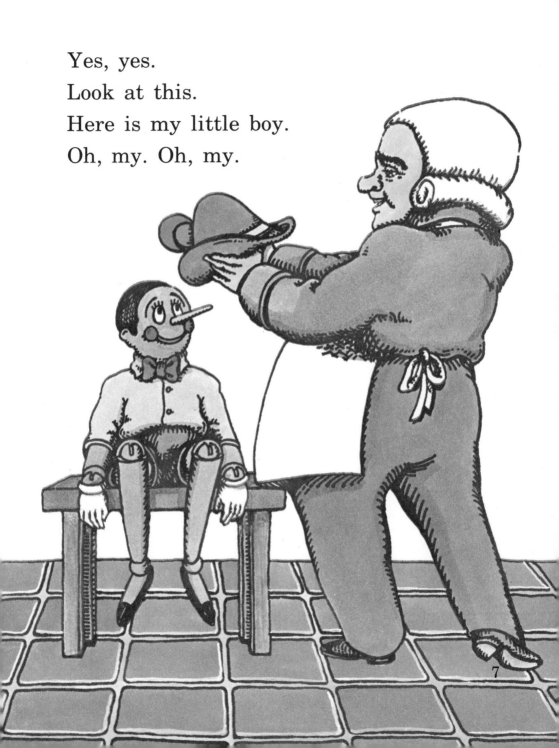

Now, little one, I want you to
go to school.
Boys and girls go to school.
Go on. Go on.
Here are books for you.

Oh, my.
Look at me.
Look at my books.
I will run to school.

No, no.

Do not go to school.

School is not fun.

Come with me to see a play.

10

Oh, I see something that
looks like me.
What fun!
What fun this is!

11

Look at you.
I want you to go with me.
Come here. Come here.

No, no, no.
I do not want to go with you.
I will run to my father.

Where did you go?
What did you do?
Where are the books?

I did not go to school.
School is not fun.
I can not find my books.

You have to go to school.
Go on. Go on.
Here is something to get
books with.

What do you have there?
You can do something good
with it.
Oh, come with us and see
what you can do.

Make it go down in here.
Down in this spot.
Good. Good.
Now go away.

Oh, my.
Now get it.
Get it out.
This is for us.
Now run, run, run with it!

Where is my little boy?
Where, oh, where?
I will go look for my boy.

Here I go.
Away, away.
Away in my boat to find
my boy.

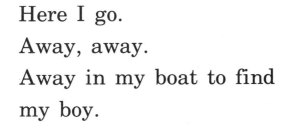

Oh, what is this?
Something big, big, big.
What will it do to me?

Oh, oh, oh.
Here I go.

Here comes something.
Look, look, look.

But what is this?
Look at me now.
What am I?
What am I?

23

Work, work, work.
I do not want to work.
I do not like this.
I want my father.

You are no good to me.
You do not work.
Get away. Get away.
Here you go.

Oh, look at me now.
But where am I?
What can I do here?

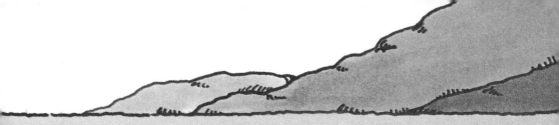

Here comes something big.
It will get me.
In I go.
In I go.
Help, help!

Father, Father.
How come you are here?
Can we get out?

I will help us get out.

Here we go!
We are out now.
We can go to the house.
Good! Good!

You did a good thing.
I will make you
into a boy.
This is how I do it!

Oh, my!
Look at me now.
Do you like me now?
I am a boy, and I want
to go to school.

31

Margaret Hillert, author of several books in the MCP Beginning-To-Read Series, is a writer, poet, and teacher.

Pinocchio uses the 72 words listed below.

a	get	no	us
am	girls	not	
and	go	now	want
are	good		way
at		oh	we
away	have	on	what
	help	one	where
big	here	out	will
boat	house		with
books	how		work
boy(s)		play	
but	I	pretty	yes
	in		you
can	into	run	
come(s)	is		
	it	school	
did		see	
do	like	something	
down	little	spot	
	look(s)		
father		that	
find		the	
for	make	there	
fun	me	thing	
funny	my	this	
		to	